THE PRETTY $\overset{the}{\wedge}$ UGLY

PALMETTO
PUBLISHING
Charleston, SC
www.PalmettoPublishing.com

Copyright © 2024 by Gabriella Smith

All rights reserved

No portion of this book may be reproduced, stored in a retrieval system, or transmitted in any form by any means—electronic, mechanical, photocopy, recording, or other—except for brief quotations in printed reviews, without prior permission of the author.

Paperback ISBN: 979-8-8229-4851-8

THE PRETTY *the* UGLY

Gabriella Smith

This book is dedicated to my sweet baby brother.

There will be no one on this planet that loves you the way I do. In time I have grown to love you unconditionally. I have understood how priceless you are to me. There are very few in this world that have a heart like you, but none have your hair, your laugh, and your sense of humor. You are so kind and gentle. You love so selflessly and that is nothing to be ashamed of. You have a brain of wonder and your spirit is something longed for by many. Everyone should feel lucky to know you. My heart goes out to you forever. I never want to see you hurt, mad, sad or lost. You deserve only the greatest things in the world and, oh how I wish I could give them to you, each and every last thing. I will never be okay with saying goodbye even on the best terms. I have loved watching you grow and I wish to see that for the rest of my life. I know in my heart you will be a great husband and father, because you are a great brother. I should be thanking the Lord for you everyday because he knew how much I needed your kindness, your sweetness, and your patience in my life.

I love you Thomas, more than our brains could fathom,
Forever.

Love, sis.

Table of Contents

THE PRETTY — 1
   Butterflies — 2
   Lies for a believer — 3
   Maybe — 4
   The Lines — 5
   Will Ya? — 6
   Touch — 7
   Promise? — 8
   Burn — 9
   If, then — 10
   Sex — 11
   Why? — 12
   Myself (Daily Affirmation) — 13
   Again but different — 14
   Even though — 15
   LMK — 16
   Dear Gabby, — 17
   Rare — 18
   Strings — 19
   From Us, For Us — 20
   If you knew — 21
   Old but New — 22
   To whom it may concern, — 23
   Kids — 24
   If we knew — 25

Show & Tell	26
Body	27
Jeans	28
Silver Springs	29
Thank you	30
What I want	31
Smile	32
Heart of Gold	33
Love me	34
Bird	35
A shower	36
Peace	37
THE UGLY	39
Tears for the River	40
Plants	41
Shadows	42
All love	43
Hate	44
Storms	45
Ice cold	46
Funeral	47
Games	48
Tear	49
That	50
Hopeless Romantic	51
Stupid	52

Choking Butterflies	53
Captivating	54
Internal conflict	55
Okay	56
Words	57
Scars	58
Wrecking Ball	59
Lost	60
Caution	61
Leave	62
Not	63
When	64
Alone	65
Not them	66
Angry	67
My mom	68
Another Man	69
My mind	70
Pathetic	71
Me & The Girls.	72
My mom II	73
Toxic	74
Cause & Effect	75
My Dad	76
Guilty	77
About the Author	78

THE PRETTY

Butterflies

Butterflies flourish there, they go wild when they hear
your voice.
I cry when I feel them dying, they live off you like oxygen.
They weep when you don't call them pretty
And they almost come out of my throat when you kiss me.
But maybe they aren't real.
I haven't felt them lately.
You've been gone so long, maybe they won't ever come back.

Where were your butterflies?
I never heard them fluttering when I got close,
I never felt the wind from their wings coming out of your
throat when our lips met.
Where were they?

Lies for a believer

Tell me you're in love.
Even though I haven't told you,
Tell me you know I'm in love and you are too.

Tell me I'm the one that makes your sky light blue
& you'll chase the sun with me all morning till noon.

Dance with me in the midnight moonlight and tell me with your eyes,
I'm the prettiest sight.

Maybe

Maybe I wasn't worthy of your love.
Maybe my laugh wasn't cute enough.
Maybe my freckles were in all the wrong places.

Maybe I called too much.
Maybe I said "I miss you" too much.
Maybe I fell in love too fast.
Maybe I didn't say the right things.

But maybe,

You never called enough.
You said "I miss you" too little.
You never wanted to fall in love.
You wanted to hear all the wrong things.

Maybe, just maybe,

You weren't worthy of my love.

The Lines

As a child coloring brought me joy.
The lines allowed me to get as close to perfection as ever.

But I threw them away when you laughed at them.

Now I only ever color outside the lines,
You hate it,
And I relish it.

Some of the most beautiful things are far from perfect.

Will Ya?

Dance with me in the rain,
Will ya?

Learn to love the rain,
Will ya?
Learn to love the smell and the feeling of it dripping off your eyelashes,
Will Ya?

We know it won't be here forever,
This feeling.
The rain.
It all goes away.
But let's learn to love it,
Will we?

Touch

It is so intoxicating.
I feel like I can't breathe around you.

My body cries for yours and I can't suppress it,
Until I have had,
ALL of you.

Just touch me.
Touch my hips.
Drive me wild.

Until I've lost all my inhibitions
And all I desire is your,

Touch.

Promise?

Dance with me.
I beg of you,
Grab my hands,
And my hips,
Slowly taste my lips.

Dancing with you is familiar.
It feels like home.
I can see the world in your eyes when you are close.
Promise me you'll never dance with another,

Promise?

Burn

Flames in my throat.
My tongue is red hot as I say your name.

Why does this feel like hell?
My skin turning blue like the hottest flame to reach earth.

Why does this feel like heaven?
Your touch is soothing,
Ice cold calming the furnace in my heart.

I burn,
But you put me out.

If, then

If its okay with you,
Then let your bed be my cell.
Keep me here,
Forever.

If its okay with you,
Then let me always be naked,
Vulnerable,
Transparent.

If its okay with you,
Then let me stay here,
And I will wait patiently for you.

If its okay with you,
Then I'll never leave.

If its okay with you,
Then this is my new home.

If its okay with you,
Then let me.

Sex

Glide your fingertips down my body.
You can go slow,
It's more than worth the wait.

Kiss my neck.
And whisper softly,
How much you want my body to melt into yours.

Make me anxious.
Make me beg.
Let me tell you how much I have longed for this,
For you,
For us.

More than sex,
Less than love.

Why?

Why do I write?
Why do I ask?
Why do I
Beg?
Plead?
Fight?
Why do I truly write?

What I say
Do,
Love,
Write,
Won't last.

So why do I even write?

For those,
Who stay up till 3 am watching someone else live their life
For those,
Who feel every emotion each one more confusing than the last
For those,
Who feel so invisible they aren't sure if they're even alive
For those,
Who feel so alone they think the oxygen leaves the room when they enter.

For those,
Know you are never alone.

Myself (Daily Affirmation)

Today will be the day I choose myself.
I choose to make today mine.
I put myself first and know,
What I did yesterday no longer belongs to me.

Only for myself,
I am me.
I dance.
I sing.
I smile.
I rest.
I eat.
I dream.
Only for myself.

I am worthy of all the love in the world.
Today,
And
Everyday onward.

Again but different

I thought I buried them so far beneath the ground,
I never wanted to see them again.

But here they are,
But this time they look different.

They are all around me.
They follow me.
The wind from their wings tickle my ears.

Are these yours?
Your butterflies?

They are different.
They are bruised and battered.
And beautiful.
I've never seen someone else's,
They go wild when I look at you.

I love your butterflies.

Even though

Tell me that even with all my
Flaws and troubles,
Even with all my
Tears and fears,
That you'll be here,
For years.

Tell me I am beautiful when I cry
Even though,
We both know why.

Just hold me and wipe my tears
Even though,
We both know it won't heal my wounds.

LMK

Let me know its okay.
Let me know we will grow,
From the pain.

Let me know it will go away.
Maybe not tomorrow or today.
But that this will disappear,
Along with this fear.

Let me know that things will be sane.
One day.

Dear Gabby,

Don't wither away in bed.

Feel the sun on your skin,
As you listen to your alt. Band.

Dance in the rain.
Don't let the moon scare you into your cage of a room.

Drive with the windows down.
Let the wind hug you,
like your mom use to.

Stop taking pictures.
Let your head play them back,
like your favorite childhood movie.

Dream of touching the sky one day.

Let the world love you unconditionally,
like your brothers do.

Let the currents pick you up,
And make you giggle,
Like your dad used to.

Let the world love you.
Like your family does.

Rare

Your name dances on my tongue.
It does pirouettes in my head.

How in all my years of breathing how have I never met someone willing to love me quite like you do?

Maybe we are both just so rare, that those before us were too weak to find the gem hidden under our dust and dirt.
But the way you look at me causes my mind to lose track of all those who have failed before you.

You, so rare,
standing like an angel.
Me, so rare,
loving you so much that just saying goodbye is painful.

Strings

I agreed to this.
Said yes knowing I couldn't foot the bill.
No strings attached.

But I can see them growing each day.
The strings.
Tethering me to you.
Your smile,
Your smell,
Just a simple caress reminds me of what we could have.
Or couldn't.

Do I stay quiet?
Do I let them grow in silence and rip them out before we get too close?
Or do I show them to you and risk having you cut them off with your sharpest words that are to come?

Do I take that leap and risk falling and breaking every part of me?
Or
Do I stay in my bubble dreaming of the air on the outside?

Why won't these go away?
Why do I want them to stay?

The strings haunt me,
Everyday.

From Us, For Us

Why can't we dance?
Sway together to our own music.

The song that rings true for us,
From us.

No rules,
nothing to follow ahead, just our hearts leading the way.

Inspiring others,
To love openly,
To hold hands tightly,
To trust fully.

Our love song for us,
From us.

If you knew

Sometimes I wish people knew my devotion.
The love I have to offer.

Sometimes I wish I didn't wear it on my sleeve so much.
Sometimes I wish people didn't take advantage or for granted.

But I think you would find comfort in it if you knew I think if you knew I love like they use to you'd sleep easier at night.

If you knew.

Old but New

Sparks,
When your skin is on mine.
All the little things we do because we are still shy.
Scared,
Because we don't know where this belongs.
Scared,
Because we don't want to move on.

We've been dancing around this for years
Yet,
We both have fears.

We can't stay here in limbo.
But promise no matter where we go,
We'll never be too far to say hello.

To whom it may concern,

I can't wait to love you.
I can't wait for all the little jokes and the tiptoes we take with each other.

I can't wait for our first fight.
For all our makeup gestures.
For the late-night binging of our show.
The staying up late just so the other doesn't fall asleep alone.

I can't wait to hear all about who you were.
And see all that you become.

To whom it may concern,
I love you.

Kids

Tell them about me.

If we knew

If only we knew the one,
He.
She.
Them.
The one.

If we knew their name, their eye color, their home
Would we run to them?
Skip straight to the ending or play the game through?

Would we still allow the wrong ones to try?
Allow memories to become scars?
Or come to the one untouched?

The wrong ones made me who I am today,
They've opened my eyes wider each time.

But if I had the choice to be with the one instantly,
would I still allow the others to misunderstand, misread,
and misconstrue the art I am.

Yes.

Show & Tell

Please show me everything.
I want to see your deepest scars.
I want to kiss all your wounds.
I know they are there.
I know they haven't fully healed.
Let me show you how worthy of love and happiness you are.

Tell me of all your sorrow.
I'll hold you close and make you feel safe.
I'll promise to never hurt you like they did.

I'll show you everything you've wanted to see.
I'll tell you everything you wanted to hear.

Body

I am so much more than my body,
I am somebody.

I have hopes,
Dreams,
Fears.
I have big, beautiful eyes
And a beautiful big heart.

I have a favorite color,
A favorite flower,
A favorite song.
But who asked?
Nobody.

But somebody will, and I'll be so excited,
To share who I am rather than,
Sharing my body.

Jeans

I remember going through a growth spurt.
Afterwards I'd be too tall for my pants, and they would just look silly on me.
So, my mom would always buy them one size up.
I'd have to wear a belt, but they worked until I grew again.

My mother was like that belt.
Holding me up until I outgrew you.
Until you and I just looked silly because,
I knew better and you couldn't change for me.

Giving away good jeans is hard,
But I knew you'd fit someone else better,
And make them feel good in their own skin.

Silver Springs

You could've watched me grow,
Watched me get help,
Watch me gain weight,
Watch me do so many things I couldn't before.

But you left before you had to cheer me on.
Before you had to see me get better.
You left before I could get better,
And now you're surprised I've changed.

Now you're surprised I don't want those things.

And I've found someone who celebrates even my smallest victories.

Thank you

When everyone has said its too hard you made it look easy.
Loving me.
You do it happily.
Thank you
For loving me.

You love me the way I use to pray for.
Softly,
Patiently.
You are sweetly
Loving me.
And here I am
Softly,
Patiently,
Sweetly,
Loving you.

Thank you for letting me love you.

What I want

If and when I can't,
Won't,
Don't have you.
I want everything that reminds me of us,
You,
This love.

I want

That couch where we fell in love.
That booth at our favorite restaurant where I truly met you for the first time.

I want

The bed where we spend countless hours exploring the landscapes of each other's bodies.

I want

Every sock that I have ever stolen from your drawers.
All the shirts that feel like you.
All the soaps that smell like you.
And all the hats that I hated so.

I want

Any small, big, significant, even minuscule thing that makes our story live on forever.
I want
It all.

I want
To hoard every piece of you so I would never have to say goodbye.

Smile

I love that smile.
The smile where your eyes close shut.
All the smiles before have made lines near your eyes and mouth.

I am thankful for those lines.
I am thankful for those before me who have made the lines.
But now
It is my turn to make them for you.

It is my turn to make your lips curl,
Your eyes squint,
And make your eyebrows raise.

It's my turn to make you
Smile.

Heart of Gold

I can see that your heart burns as hot as mine.
I can see that you love to love.

I hope all those before me didn't take all your spark, hope, and love.

Even if they did, I hope to bring it all back to you.
I can so clearly see you were once like me.
I just hope I remind you of who you used to be.

Love me

Love me loudly,
But speak to me softly.

Be quick to adore me,
But slow to leave me.

Love me madly,
But keep me sane.

Have my back,
And never turn yours.

Let "I love you" be easy,
And "goodbye" be hard.

Bird

You have taught me so many things.

To keep my chin up,
To speak my mind,
But keep my peace.

To love selflessly,
But never lose myself.

Live honestly,
But protect my privacy.

To spread my wings,
And,
Find where the birds sing.

A shower

I feel most beautiful after a shower.
My skin still flushed from the red-hot water washing all my blues away.

I can cry in the shower and the faucet will cry with me.
The steam surrounds me in the warmest hug.
The tub holds me just fine,
And it never asks me to be anything but naked.

I love
A shower.

Peace

There is peace in harmony,
Not in silence,
Because being alone is terrifying.

THE UGLY

Tears for the River

The song you sang to her you sang to me.
You said you'd call but you never rang me.
These tears aren't for you
Or for me.
They are for the river.

Only for the forest to see
Only for the forest to hear me weep.

These tears aren't for you.

Plants

My tree so tall and strong,
Delivering the one thing I absolutely need.
Always protecting me from the sun,
And the storms from the outside world.

But you never saw me as a flower,
More like this inconvenient weed hanging on to your roots.
Something so truly annoying you'd pay to see me wilt.

Why can't I be your flower?
I promise to grow where you please.
I promise to be your favorite color,
And only grow in your favorite season.
Let me be your flower.
Please.

Shadows

Why do you hide me away?
Why do you keep me locked up with your heart?
Why can't I come into the light?
I won't outshine you.
I just want to show your heart beating in my hands.
You kiss me under covers and tell me to disappear when the sun comes up.

When I asked why you told me,
Only stars shine in the darkness,
And love only happens in the shadows.

All love

Behind the smiles is all love truly heartbreaking?
Just like that of my parents?

All give, no take.
I give all,
Time,
Thoughts,
Soul,
My life.
Only to feel more than lonely.
Worthless,
Invisible,
And just plain wrong.

Who am I right for?
Maybe no one.

Hate

Let me go.
No, tell me to go.
No, make me go.

Push me out the door,
Down your steps,
Laugh at me as I beg you to stop.

Call me ugly,
Unlovable,
Unbearable.

Make me cry,
Make me hate.

So maybe I can hate you as much as I hate myself for loving you.

Please.

Storms

I am a storm.
Exciting to watch,
Perfect for slow days.

You love the rain when it hasn't been there for ages.
But soon you grow tired of the rain,
And remember that the sunshine exists.

So I pass,
But I come back when you ask.

You could love the sun forever,
But never the rain.

Ice cold

When did we learn that being cool meant showing less interest?

Not just in school,
But in love.
Breaking hearts makes you wildly desirable.

Not calling back means being called a heartthrob.
Not texting back means I'll love you more.

Never showing feelings means I get all the feels.

If this makes you cool,
Baby you're ice cold.

Funeral

Here we are dressed in black.

I brought my heart,
And you brought her.

We all mourn differently,
But I guess you do yours under the covers.

The open casket showed the butterflies,
But there was only one set.
Mine.

Games

Do you wanna play these games?

I'll lay down the cards,
Go all in,
And show you my hearts.

I guess you won,
Because I'm still sitting at the table,
Hoping you'll come back,
And play fair this time.

Tear

I could feel the wounds resurfacing,
as you touched my skin again.

Each kiss made my eyes water.

A tear fell into the tear,
And it burned all over again.

Why did I let you have me again?
I feel sick.
Sick of you holding me.

That

Why?
Why did you have to say that?

I wanted to leave it unspoken.
I didn't want to acknowledge that.

Maybe its true,
But maybe its too early.

Don't say that.
"I love you"
No, don't say that.

Hopeless Romantic

I possibly cherish what we have
Too much.
Maybe its truly not as grand as I think it is.
Maybe I romanticize it
Too much.

Stupid

Loving you was stupid,
But I never played dumb.
It was genuine,
And complicated.
Wouldn't trade it for the world.

You weren't ready,
And I was more than.

I wanted communication,
And time.
And you were only trying to make me happy with false hope.

Choking Butterflies

I can feel them dying.
I can feel them gasping for you.
But I can't provide for them.

They're evil,
Sinical,
I'm afraid of what they have become.

They make me miserable.
But do I blame you,
Or myself?

I don't know.

Most likely myself,
I know the butterflies will.

But I can't allow them to flutter for you.
You just aren't worthy.
They deserve better.

Captivating

I am not unique.
I am not different.
I am not remarkable.
Or even at all captivating.

To you at least.

The only time I am more than a passing thought is the mere twenty minutes you spend gawking at my body while thrusting your parts into me.

But why on this earth would I expect to have your undivided attention with clothes on.

Because I am not unique,
Different,
Remarkable,
Or even the slightest bit captivating.

Internal conflict

My third drink,
I don't remember asking for,
But I guess I did.

My shorts,
I don't remember being too short,
But I guess they were.

Wasn't this what I wanted?
Not just to be a passing, fleeting moment.
To be seen,
To be heard,
By someone older,
More mature.

But you,
Was not what I asked for.

The touching,
The groping,
The kiss.

I am not an object,
But you made me one.
Complete with personification,
Which none of this I asked for.

So why was it okay?

Maybe my shorts were too short,
Maybe I did drink too much.
But I never asked for this.

Okay

I am not in love with who I am,
Or what I have done.
I wear makeup so I don't look like myself.
So I don't look like that girl,
Who is less than,
Small,
Inferior.

But somehow I still feel like the most unwanted thing on this earth.
Yes, thing.
Because I have allowed others to shape me,
And mold me into a
Thing.

I am not okay.

Words

Those nasty words.
They penetrate my taste buds.
My tongue bleeds until I cough them out.
Ugly,
Filthy,
Words.

"Failure, skinny, slut, unlovable, crazy."

Scars

I am covered in scars of words,
Fears,
And regrets.

Can you find beauty in the scary,
In the strange,
In the shortchange?

Can you heal me?
Or do you just want to feel me?
Do you want to steal from me?
Do you even see me?

Do you hear me?
I'm screaming,
Shouting,
Belting,
For acknowledgement.
For commitment.

Just see me,
Hear me,
Hold me.

Wrecking Ball

You broke down confidence that I have spent years of building in a matter of seconds.
You have shattered all the faith I had in the world.
You broke my heart even before I let you hold it.

Lost

I have lost everything.
Even all the things I never had.

Me.
One thing I'll never achieve is my own identity.
The longer I am alive, the further away I am from myself.

Voice.
I can't speak loud enough to ask for help.
A crack escapes from my mouth, and then a hand covers it.
My mother's?
My significant other's?
More times than not it is my own.

Hope.
I've stopped eating.
I'd rather sleep the day away and feel fulfilled from my own fantasy than food.
Its easier to let people, love, happiness, the whole damn world pass me by than to open my eyes and get out of bed.

Caution

I used to beg for a call.
Now I fear it because there is no telling what will come out.
There is no telling which side of me will answer.
But why do you deserve the sweet side?

You don't.
Don't call.
Ever.

Leave

The things that reside in my mind without benefit to me are awfully daring.
Like him,
Or him,
Or the other him.
And their words,
Their scents,
Their taste in music
Their touch.

They are being banished.
They deserve no part of me, not a single piece.
Not my present, nor my future.
The only place they can float around is in the past.
And I do not say this kindly,
Leave.

We are no longer tethered together.
I grew,
I grow,
I am growing without your "reassurance".
I know I'm doing good,
I know I am standing taller,
Without your "support".
I am not saying this kindly,
Leave.

Just because you were here once doesn't mean you still have the key,
Because I changed the lock on my heart.
I will never say this kindly,
Leave.

Not

Maybe I am not the one you fall in love with.
Maybe I am not the one people settle down with.
But I'm so tired of not being loved.

I'm so tired of not being enough,
Even though I am more than enough to begin with.

You've been broken,
Beat down,
Taken for granted.
But how can you do that to someone like me?

Yes, I'm not the one.
Not the one who deserves to be hurt.

When

When will they stop disappointing me?
When will my standards be met?
When can I stop loving so hard?
When can I stop holding on so tightly?
When will I give myself a second to breathe?

Alone

Sometimes I feel like I have no one.
There's such a void,
A time in between all the chaos in my life that I feel so lost,
So alone.

I feel like I don't even have myself,
Because who even am I?
Alone, that's who.

I feel like I'm too busy learning about everyone else,
And I slowly take pieces of them as they pass through.

But without those pieces,
Those people,
I am alone.

These voids don't last long enough for me to find myself.
I feel like the world is happening around me,
And I'm just a board piece.

How can no one see how alone I am?
Please don't leave me all
Alone.

Not them

Trust me I get it.
I have a target on my back,
My armor is enticing,
It screams "pick me"
And you did.

You took away so much.
But today I know,
Because I'm such a threat,
Because I fight and question every fiber of your existence,
and remind you how small you are.
You hate it,
No, you love it.
Because no one has ever talked down to you,
Because no one has challenged you before.

I said no, and you heard,
"make me like it."

So yeah I understand me.
I was strong enough to not hate you, I was strong enough to act like you didn't exist.
But I don't understand them.
What if they aren't strong enough?
What if you ruined their life,
Or made them end it?
Don't hurt them.

I understand me,
But not them.

Angry

Sometimes I hate everyone,
And everything.
I want nothing,
And no one.
I want everyone to feel as alone as I do.

I could hurt you,
I could scream,
I could show you how hot I burn.
But then you'd just call me crazy.

So how is it fair that I sit here hating everything,
And have to swallow it all by myself?
I really can't anymore.

I hate you,
And I wish I never met anyone.

My mom

I'll never understand how she bears the weight of all the love she has for my father.

She and him are both remarried now.
And she is forced to bear that weight under layers of shame,
And the title of a wife of another.

I truly believe that this weight will kill her,
And sadly, not quick enough to ease her soul.

I am one of the few she shares these feelings to,
Even fewer I am one who is understanding of those feelings.

My heart weeps for her indefinitely.

I am sorry mom,
That you are forced to love my dad in the dark.
But I will always sit in the dark with you and hold you.
I love you.

Another Man

Here I am again writing about another man that I bleed my heart out for.
And then wonder why I feel so empty, they never give me something to fill myself with.
The pain can make you doubt love,
And life.
I want something so beautiful,
I want unconditional burning love.

And I think I settle for you because you are nice.

My mind

Thoughts,
Voices,
Memories,
Ideas,
My mind.

Weaponized against me.

My mind hates my heart,
My lungs,
My lips,
Me.
My mind hates me,
And I hate it.

Does he even love me?
Am I ugly,
Sad,
Crazy?

It's all in your head,
It's all in my head,
I know.

Pathetic

My head is pounding,
My eyes are red.

My mascara rolls down my face,
Like my begging rolls out of my mouth,
Pathetically.

Please listen to me.
Pathetic.
Please don't shout at me.
Pathetic.
Please don't leave me.
Pathetic.
Please just hold me.
Pathetic.

I just want you to lick the wounds you caused.
Pathetic.

Why won't you fix the problems you caused?
I swear I'll forgive and forget if you just say sorry.
Pathetic.

Please just say sorry.
Pathetic.

Me & The Girls.

You stormed out.
And we're waiting.
Me & the girls.

We all beg for your attention.
Me & the girls.

We all love you.
Me & the girls.

My mom II

I'll never understand how she bears the weight of all the love she has for my father.

They both made their beds,
But the difference is most of the time she lies in hers awake,
In the dead of night reminiscing,
Crying,
Questioning, maybe one day?
While her now husband snores just loud enough allowing her to cry without being noticed.

Eventually she begs the sun to come up,
So she can begin pretending for the day.

Her days must be busy,
Or the darkness where she loves my father openly calls her so sweetly.
She truly hates the predicament she is in.

The world around her forces her to "move on".
Some would believe she is a weak,
Sad woman living in the past.

But they would be horribly wrong.
She is one of the strongest people I know.

Toxic

I'm so toxic.
I hate you for going out,
And having a good time without me.

I'm jealous of the people who get to see you smile,
Angry at you for making fond memories absent of me.
Why am I so toxic?

Cause & Effect

I sleep in my makeup,
And wonder why I have acne.
I eat candy,
And wonder why I have cavities.
I push everyone away,
And wonder why I am so alone.

My Dad

I can't blame you for what you didn't know when I was little.
I know you tried,
And I know raising a girl isn't easy.
I know losing your tomboy wasn't easy.
I know seeing me give my heart away countless times
wasn't easy.
I know knowing nothing about me wasn't easy.

But I do blame you,
For thinking the distance between us was easier.

Guilty

I feel guilty for not spending enough time with people,
My dad,
My mom,
My brothers,
My grandma,
My boyfriend.

I feel guilty for spending too much time with people,
My dad,
My mom.
My brothers,
My grandma,
My boyfriend.

I feel guilty that my relationship with some hurt others.

I feel guilty that my relationship with others hurts some.

I don't know how to absolve myself from this guilt.
Maybe someone else should.
All I know is I hate it.

I have to put everyone in a box,
And serve them the same time as others.
Otherwise I'm a bad person with no regard for anyone.
Otherwise I'm guilty.

About the Author

I am 21 years old, I work as a Bartender in Sumter SC. I am diagnosed with Bi-Polar Disorder II. I love to write, listen to music, and enjoy time with my dog Dixie.

I am the middle child sandwiched between two brothers and I love every minute of it.

www.ingramcontent.com/pod-product-compliance
Lightning Source LLC
LaVergne TN
LVHW042156070526
838201LV00047BA/1427